MW01195082

The Elitch Gardens Story
Memories of Jack Gurtler

by Corinne Hunt
Jack Gurtler

Editorial and Production Coordination
O.J. Seiden

A Rocky Mountain Writers Guild Publication

2969 Baseline Rd.
Boulder, Colorado 80303

Copyright © 1982
Corinne Hunt & Jack Gurtler
All rights reserved
Library of Congress Catalogue
Card number 82-80241
ISBN 0-937050-27-X
Composed, printed, and bound in U.S.A.

Typesetting and layout by
Kenton & Associates
Denver, Colorado

DEDICATION

To my brother, "Budd" and my nephew, "Sandy" — Arnold B. Gurtler, Jr. and Arnold S. Gurtler — who are carrying on the fine traditions of Elitch Gardens that have always made it true that "Not to See Elitch's is Not to See Denver."

EDITOR'S NOTE:

When I first became involved with this project I had no idea what a delight it would turn out to be. It wasn't long before I realized that **The Elitch Gardens Story** was in fact the story of Denver. "Not To See Elitch's Is Not To See Denver" is much more truth than advertising slogan. Elitch's is the pulse of Denver. As the stories began to unfold before me I was amazed at how well the people who have been Elitch's for almost a century have understood the mood and needs of Denverites. The nostalgia of Elitch's is the nostalgia of Denver. In an effort to keep the warmth and love that Jack Gurtler has for his park and the people of Denver, Corinne Hunt and I have tried to keep as much of his language in the book as possible. I hope we have succeeded in bringing you the same joy we had in collecting the information for this book, **The Elitch Gardens Story . . . .**

Othniel J. Seiden
Editor

Jack Gurtler . . .
He has had a lifelong love affair
with Elitch's and Denver.

Jack Gurtler, Chairman of the Board, who spent some 50 years in the family-owned enterprise tells us his personal memories in the Elitch Garden Story.

Special Photos by Brad Gordon

INTRODUCTION

The beat is today, the sound of modern America at play. That's the way it's always been — contemporary — for almost 100 years. It seems almost inconceivable that any spot as lively as Elitch Gardens on a hot summer's night could be old, could have a century of stories to tell, but if the old apple trees could talk, what tales they would recount.

They remember lions — and bears, camels, and an ostrich that pulled a sulky. They remember Sarah Bernhardt, and Douglas Fairbanks, Sr. and all the Big Bands that ever traveled the country.

The apple trees can't talk, but a man who has known Elitch Gardens for the whole of his lifetime can, and so, Jack Gurtler tells us "The Elitch Gardens Story."

The old auto entrance. The price of admission was based on the number in the cars and sometimes young people would hide in the back seat to avoid being counted. Then in the winter, they'd have a change of heart and would send the admission price in letters addressed "Dear Mr. Elitch". When the greenhouse gave way to more parking space, the practice of admission by the car was abolished.

THE BEGINNING

Hunt: Of course, we know that you weren't there in person at the beginning, Jack, but you've lived with the Elitch Garden story all of your life so it must seem that you were there. Just how did Elitch Gardens get started?

Gurtler: John Elitch came to Denver in 1880 from San Francisco where he'd run a restaurant in one of the theatre buildings. Lots of actors and actresses frequented his place, so he developed quite an interest in the theatre and when he sold the eating place, he invested in a traveling show with some other people and lost his money.

When he came to Denver he was broke, but he started working in restaurants again and finally opened one of his own. It was down on Arapahoe Street and was called the Tortoni.

His wife, Mary, whom he'd married when she was only 16 and he was 20, was a good helpmate, and they bought an acreage in northwest Denver to raise vegetables for their restaurant.

The property had belonged to some people named Chilcott, who had planted quite an apple orchard, so it was a beautiful place when the trees bloomed in the spring. John and Mary Elitch began to improve the place. John wanted to give Denver a spot to compare with the Woodward gardens he remembered from San Francisco.

Mary Elitch and the goats that were part of the early zoological garden from which Elitch's grew.

Mary Elitch and the ostrich she trained to pull a cart. This was such a remarkable thing that photos of the pair were published all over the world.

Mary Elitch and the lion cubs. One of these became the model for the lions at the Chicago Art Institute.

Well, among his friends was P.T. Barnum of the circus and he wintered some of his circus animals and equipment down around Sloan's Lake. When too many babies were born to his circus animals, Barnum gave some of them to John Elitch. When the Gardens opened on May 1, 1890, they were called Elitch's Zoological Gardens.

Hunt: It must have been an exciting day for Denver, that opening day.

Gurtler: Oh my yes! I've read accounts of it. It was cloudy and threatened to rain, but people turned out. Remember, this was way out in the country in those days and they had to ride what they called "the old Berkley motor" or streetcar, and I guess it really got a workout that day.

There was a cafe — the old Orchard Cafe building that we just tore down for the 1981 season — and a soda fountain booth and a confectionery pavillion. And the animals — bears, lions, a camel and much more. There was a band, of course — there's always been bands and music at Elitch's — and the old accounts say that one bear would dance a waltz style everytime the band struck up a lively tune.

Barnum and his wife were there, and Mr. and Mrs. Tom Thumb. He was the famous midget, you know. And the Mayor of Denver made a speech.

But it was the theatre performance — a whole series of vaudeville acts — that really got the crowd settled down. And that was in the same theatre that stands there today. It's the only original building still left on the grounds.

Hunt: But didn't John Elitch die soon after the Gardens opened?

Gurtler: Yes, unfortunately he did. He died out in San Francisco in March, 1891. When the Gardens closed after that first season, he organized a minstrel troup, the Elitch, Schilling and Goodyear Minstrels, and while they were on tour in San Francisco, John Elitch got pneumonia and died.

Hunt: So Mary had to carry on alone?

Gurtler: Yes; she was as interested in the Gardens as John had been and was determined to make their dreams for it come true.

She was good with the animals. She'd trained an ostrich to pull a sulky in which she rode around the park. It's said that photographs of this remarkable pair were printed in newspapers in London, Vienna, Paris, and even Calcutta. The ostrich, poor thing, died a horrible death. Some clown of a traveling salesman fed him celluloid advertising buttons!

There are other pictures of her with the lion cubs on a leash, and down in the pit with the bears.

One of the lions, by the way became the model for the great guardian lions outside the Chicago Art Institute He was supposed to have been a perfect specimen of lion — head, body, everything in perfect configuration.

But Mary was also pretty savvy about the theatre. The first few seasons after John's death she presented the best vaudeville obtainable, and light opera. Then she organized her own stock company and the first performance on May 30, 1897, was "Helene" followed by "A Bachelor's Romance."

5

Mary Elitch and the bears in the bear pit. One of the bears, Dewey, missed Mary so much when she was on her honeymoon that he went to her house to find her and cut his throat trying to get in through a window. The headlines were *"Dewey the bear, commits suicide."*

During the construction period, James O'Neill, who was Eugene O'Neill's father, had stopped by to see his old friend, John Elitch, and promised to return some day to act in a play in John's theatre. Although John was dead, Mr. O'Neill came back to play the leading man during that 1897 season.

George Edeson was the first director of the stock company and laid down a rule that was followed by my grandfather, my father, and my brother and me as long as we operated a stock company. That was that the members of the company must be artists of experience.

Hunt: What were some of the other "firsts" that Elitch's was famous for in Mary Elitch's day?

Gurtler: Well, it was the first place in the West that showed Edison's Warograph. These animated pictures were the great grand daddy of all the movies, and they really created a sensation when they came to Denver.

It was during the Spanish-American War, of course, and Elitch's had flower beds depicting the American and Cuban flags.

Mary produced "Cyrano de Bergerac" the first time it was played in Denver. It required a cast of 100. And she brought Sarah Bernhardt to Denver in 1906 to play "Camille" at a matinee and "La Sorcier" at the evening performance.

Hunt: Didn't Mary Elitch marry again?

Gurtler: Yes, she married Thomas D. Long in 1900. He was her box office manager. But he died in 1906 and she never married again. She managed the park herself.

Hunt: It must have been quite a feat for a woman in those days. Did she continue to do well?

Gurtler: She did, for a number of years, but when things began to slide as she got older, the Elitch Gardens story opened another chapter.

JOHN M. MULVIHILL

Hunt: This new chapter in The Elitch Gardens Story must have to do with your family getting involved.

Gurtler: Yes, and it began with my grandfather, John Michael Mulvihill. He'd come to Denver in 1902 from Pennsylvania where he'd had about three careers, first as a teacher, then as a penologist working in the Pennsylvania reformatory at Huntingdon, and lastly, as an executive in the Carnegie Steel Mills.

But then he developed a lung condition which was described as incurable, and like so many others did in those days, he came out to Colorado for the fine, pure mountain air, and got well.

Robert W. Speer, who was one of Denver's great mayors, was a lifelong friend of my grandfather's and he introduced him to the officers of the old Denver Gas and Electric Company. They hired him to take charge of credit and collections.

Grandfather was somewhat politically minded and he frequently met with some of his political cronies down at old Tom O'Connell's place about Fourteenth and Larimer. Tom was from Pennsylvania too, and like Grandfather,

John M. Mulvihill, Jack and Budd's grandfather and the first of four generations to be involved in Elitch Gardens.

came to Denver with a lung condition. He became quite a guy around town and he'd land in jail every so often. His friend, my grandfather, would bail him out.

Tom had this place called The Blue Goose, and that's why he'd get put in jail. Because behind the candy bars and the sandwiches and the soda pop were his living quarters, and more important, it was where he brewed his own stuff — beer, whiskey, and everything else.

So Grandfather would get together with the fellows over at Tom's place and he got interested in city affairs. The fellows said, "John, why don't you run for the schoolboard?" He thought pretty good of that, so soon there were pictures and billboards and pamphlets all around the city — "John M. Mulvihill for Schoolboard."

Well, in those days, there were three things that could be terrible for a fellow and Grandfather had all three. He was Irish, Catholic and a Democrat.

There was quite an active Ku Klux Klan in Denver and they found out where John Mulvihill lived (all of us — Grandfather and Grandmother, Dad, Mother, Budd and I and usually some visiting aunts or uncles — lived together at 3814 Newton.) Grandfather got word that the Klan was going to come over and burn a cross on our lawn. His idea was that all of us should go to the basement, turn out all the lights and make it look like we were not at home. Maybe that would turn 'em off the notion, and apparently it did — they didn't burn a cross. But, unfortunately, the power of the Klan defeated my Grandfather from getting on the schoolboard.

Grandpa bought the Gardens in 1916. I'd like to tell you how he bought it and why he bought it.

In the years before 1916, Mary Elitch, as you know, had married John Long and after a few years he died, leaving Mary all alone. She was very capable and still had the desire that she and her first husband, John Elitch, had in their dreams. She continued to try to do things in the Gardens; she did quite well and kept it up some, but one thing she forgot to do was pay her bills.

In the early 1900's there were a few very important business men here in Denver who knew of Elitch's — had been out here as patrons many times, and thought it was a very beautiful thing that should be continued. They also knew John Mulvihill was very capable, so they decided they'd better send him out to see what was going on because they'd learned that among other things that Mary Elitch forgot to pay were her taxes, and it was likely the property would be sold to satisfy that obligation.

They knew of a man here in Denver by the name of F.G. Bonfils who was running the great Denver Post. He was feared by a lot of people here in Denver and had a lot of enemies, yet he had a lot of good friends, too, including my grandfather.

Well, anyway these men thought it would be a shame if F.G. Bonfils got ahold of the Gardens, because he had a controlling interest in a circus, started

Balloon ascensions were big entertainment in the Gay Nineties. Ivy Baldwin was a big favorite at the Gardens. That's Mary Elitch next to the bearded gentleman.

Yes, there was once a lake at Elitch Gardens. Mary Elitch is out for a little row on the lake.

**Arnold B. Gurtler
Jack and Budd's dad.**

here in Denver, the Sells-Floto Circus Company, and they didn't want him to get the Gardens because they were afraid he'd turn it into a circus camp and it would just go to the dickens.

So they got John Mulvihill from the Old Gas and Electric Company and said to him, "John, we want you to go out to Elitch's and see what kind of financial shape it is in."

John said, "I don't know how an amusement park is supposed to figure on the books." But they insisted he go out and check so he did, taking his Saturdays and Sundays off from the Gas & Electric Company. He reported back that it was in terrible shape; that the bills hadn't been paid and that there were a lot of dunning letters in the files, and worst of all, that the taxes were in arrears.

So these men bought the Gardens and then they told my grandfather that they wanted him to go out and run it for them!

Well, my Grandfather, God love him, said, "Look, fellows. I did what you asked me to do, but as for running an amusement area or a zoo out there, I don't know anything about that kind of a business." But they insisted, and so Grandfather operated it for these fellows for awhile, and then, he finally bought them out and he was the sole owner of the World Famous Elitch Gardens Amusement Park.

By that time, my Father, Arnold B. Gurtler, Sr., had married John Mulvihill's daughter, Marie. He was working at the great old Denver Dry Goods Department store in the decorating department. Like my grandfather had been, he was only interested in Elitch Gardens as a guest and a spectator, but Grandpa needed his help.

As Grandfather had before, he became sole owner. My Dad spent his weekends at the Park, working to help get it back in shape.

In those days there was a wooden fence all around the Park, and it was in pretty bad shape. Grandfather said to his son-in-law, "Arnold, I want you to get a bucket of nails and a couple of hammers and you and John Sachs go around and tighten up all those boards that are falling down."

So Dad and John Sachs, who had worked for Mary Elitch, went out and spent a couple of weekends pounding in nails. Then my Dad went to Grandpa and said, 'Dad,'' (he always called his father-in-law "Dad.") "Dad, this fence-fixing is a bunch of hooey. Everytime I pound in one nail, two more jump out. What are we ashamed of? Let's tear all that wood down and put up a link fence of some kind and let the people look in to see what we've got here."

And that was done. It was one of the earliest improvements my Grandfather made at the Gardens.

Marie Mulvihill Gurtler, Jack and Budd's mother.

Mary Elitch and her first home in the gardens.

The fine brick home that John Mulvihill built on the grounds for Mary Elitch.

They went along like that for awhile, my Father working on weekends, and then my Grandfather said: "Son, I'm going to need you all the time out here. I quit the gas company and I'm out here all the time, and you try to come out nights when we're open in the summer, and spend your weekends here in the winter. Let's both give it our full attention and I think we can do something pretty special with this place."

So my Dad quit the Denver Dry Goods Company and became part of the family operation of Elitch Gardens. My Grandfather and Dad, Grandfather's wife, Catherine, and my Father's wife, Marie, were all stockholders with my father having the least amount of stock.

When Grandfather bought the gardens in 1916, he said to Mary Elitch Long: "Mrs. Long, as long as you live we would be proud to have you live here in your regular home here in the Gardens." She did for many years, and finally Grandfather told her, "Mrs. Long, you know your old home is getting quite bad. I want to build you a new home here. You go down and live at the Cosmo — (then still called the Metropole — which my Grandfather had an interest in) and we'll put up a new house for you." Which he did — a beautiful brick home with a number of bedrooms — and he installed the very first gas and electric stove in all of North Denver for his friend, Mary Elitch Long.

So Mary lived there until her later, senile years. We called her Aunt Mary. I was very fond of her, and she used to take my brother and me into her home that Grandfather had built for her. There was a solarium and in this solarium she had many things she'd acquired on her trips around the world. And we were always intrigued with these little models and things.

In the 1930's when my brother and I were ushering in the theatre — one of our first numerous jobs we had in the Park — Mary Elitch always had the first two lower boxes on the far right of the theatre. And between them, they held 14 seats, 7 seats in each box as they still do. They are seldom sold today.

Most everytime in those years, Mary Elitch would come in with a bunch of people numbering 20 or more, and there weren't that many seats in the boxes, so we ushers had to do the best we could by placing her friends wherever we could in the seats that weren't occupied. This could be quite a problem, but she was such a charming lady that we always did our best for her.

Ushers at the Elitch Theatre. Jack Gurtler is 9th from the left.

15

GROWING UP IN AN AMUSEMENT PARK

Hunt: You and your brother literally grew up in the Park, didn't you?

Gurtler: Yes, I suppose we really did. The family all lived just down the street at 3814 Newton Street, and the Gardens became the playground, not just for Budd and me, but for all the gang of boys we grew up with there in North Denver.

We did some crazy things, I can tell you! The Gardens used to have "Frontier Days" celebrations on the big summer holidays — 4th of July and Labor Day, and somehow we wound up with a miniature stage coach to be used in the parades.

Grandfather had bought us a set of ponies, and the park owned some young horses to drive in these Frontier Day parades and to haul soil down from up around Golden for use in the greenhouses — to grade the baseball field and chores like that.

Well, one day — a Saturday or a Wednesday — matinee day at the Theatre — we hitched up our ponies and about 4 small horses to this stagecoach, and kind of meandered around up by the old figure 8 roller coaster. Some of the gang rode inside and either Budd or I was driving with the other one riding shotgun. It was what they call a 6-rein hitch, with three reins in each hand.

The main entrance, from 38th and Tennyson.

A scene few people see — Elitch Gardens in the winter.

It's hard to imagine, when summer brings out the flowers and the rides and the crowds that Elitch's ever experiences winter.

The old gate at 38th and Tennyson — this was probably the cover for a program announcing the School of the Theatre and Dance which was a big part of the summer program at the Gardens for many years.

The Wildcat is deserted and the statue looks cold in this winter picture.

This is the crew that built the 38th and Tennyson gate that had to give way to the "progress" of widening 38th Avenue.

Workmen building the main gate at 38th and Tennyson. This gate had to be removed when 38th Avenue was widened and the present gate was built.

The gate at 38th and Tennyson which had to be removed for the widening of 38th Avenue.

The Carousel that was replaced in the early 20's. This one is still delighting people in Kit Carson County in eastern Colorado.

Well, like ponies and horses do, when we turned the team around, they got wind of the oats and hay waiting for them in their barn over where the greenhouses are now, and they took off like a bat from you know where. Down the front walk, between the Troc and the candy stand they went, completely out of control, and headed straight for the theatre, just as the ladies were coming out for intermission. Those ladies scattered like scared ducks as the ponies flew by. And there was Grandfather, standing by the box office!

You never saw kids unhitch horses faster than we did. We rubbed 'em down and put the coach away because, scared as we were of Grandfather over the runaway, we were more scared not to take the proper care of the horses in the way we'd been taught we must do. And then we ran home faster than those horses had gone by the theatre. Grandfather was there ahead of us, however, with his 3-strop razor strop ready and we got what we probably deserved!

My grandfather ordered a carousel from the Philadelphia Toboggan Company in about 1925 to replace the one Mary Elitch had installed in 1905. That original carousel, by the way, still exists out in Kit Carson County on the eastern plains of Colorado.

Anyway, it took 3 years for the new ride to be built, with its 67 hand carved horses and chariots, and while it was being made in Pennsylvania, Elitch Gardens was busy building a building to house it in.

The boys in our gang were great bicycle enthusiasts and we'd ride around and around the huge circular floor, pretending we were racers, and lots of times we'd get dizzy and crash our bikes into the wall. If we broke a wheel, we'd save up our money and get 'em fixed without telling our dad about it.

One adventure with our bikes had far-reaching consequences that came back to haunt us when we were grown men and operating the park after our father had retired.

I suppose it was one of my wild ideas — I was full of them in those days! All the building roofs from the Trocadero all around the park were pretty well connected, with covered walkways between.

Well, one day I said to the fellows, "Hey, wouldn't it be swell to get our bikes up on the roofs and see how far around the park we can ride?"

Of course the guys went for it, and we found some rope and a couple of others and I got up on the roof and pulled all the bikes up and we rode all over the place, having a real ball.

Well, in later years we had to replace a lot of those roofs and some of the problems seemed to tie in with the damage our bikes had caused. It cost us a lot of money and seemed as though our childhood prank had come home to roost.

Of course, it wasn't all play in the Gardens, even for kids. We had to work, too. We sold cushions in the old grandstand my father built for the baseball field.

This is a detail of design from the Carousel.

The former offices of the Gardens facing 38th Avenue. The old smokestack for the greenhouses can be seen near the right of the photo. The entrance to the Theatre boxoffice now occupies some of this location.

The great midway with the Penny Arcade and The Old Mill (which later burned) prominent.

An older view of the Orchard Cafe. The porches were added to make a pleasant spot to dine out doors.

Another one of the great annual picnics — the Denver Lodge No. 3, S.E.A.

This was the **D.&R.G.W.** picnic at Elitch Gardens in 1927. Company picnics are still a big treat at the Gardens, after the regular season.

The old Orchard Cafe, last of the original buildings except the theatre. Nate Boggio ran it the year this photo was taken. It's gone now but like the Trocadero, it lives on in the memories of those who enjoyed dining there before the theatre.

The formal gardens viewed from the air.

All ages enjoy Elitch Gardens. This crowd was waiting for the drawing for bicycles given away on a special holiday weekend.

A publicity shot of Hop-A-Long and his horse.

The Old Mill dark ride. Unfortunately, this was the scene of a tragic fire a few years later.

Hop-A-Long Cassidy came to Elitch's, too, and brought out a huge crowd of admiring fans.

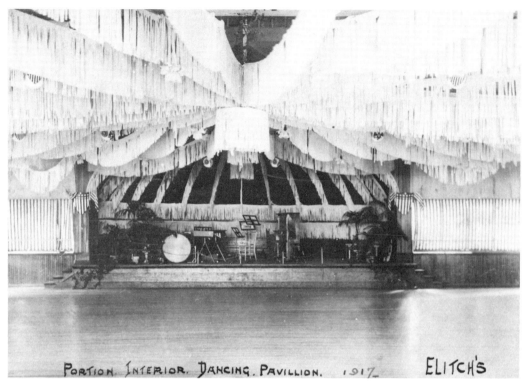

PORTION. INTERIOR. DANCING. PAVILLION.   1917.   ELITCH'S

This is the way the Trocadero looked in 1917.

The beautiful Trocadero Ballroom. It lives on in the memories of countless couples who danced there.

26

The Summer Round-up of the National Association of Amusement Parks, Resorts and Beaches at Elitch's in 1952.

My dad was crazy about baseball. They'd always had baseball at the Gardens, even in Mary Elitch's time, but my father formed a league. It was 5 teams, of which one was the Elitch Gardens team.

In the beginning there was no grandstand, just a few benches along side, so our father built a grandstand that would hold about a thousand people. It even had a roof to provide shade, and the seats had backs so people could be comfortable.

Budd and I were bat boys, and then we'd sell cushions, and the Park had a couple of hawkers selling candy and popcorn. The admission — I think it was about 50¢ — went to the umpires.

We liked to go out there after early Mass on Sunday when the men were getting the ground ready. The all-night man would have soaked it down with a big fire hose, and then it had to be harrowed, because it got so hard packed from the cars parking there during the week.

And after it was harrowed, it had to be smoothed with a drag. All this was done with horse-drawn machines, and we boys could ride on the harrow and the drag.

Neither us boys nor our father wanted to go home for Sunday dinner. It must have been hard on our mother and our grandmother, getting a big Sunday dinner ready and all of us more interested in baseball than in eating dinner.

These are some of the things I remember about being a kid with a whole amusement park to play in.

The baseball league teams that played at the Gardens in the 20's. Note the two young fellows just to the right of the fellow kneeling in front of the Elitch Team. In the Elitch uniform, bat boys, Jack and Budd Gurtler!

This was the La Fonda Pavillion set for a special dinner. It was removed in 1980 to make way for a new ride.

Fryer Hill, in the winter. Fryer Hill is named for that place in Leadville, in honor of our father, who grew up there. The booths are all named for mines in the area.

Another winter scene of the Gardens.

This was the old North Picnic Pavillion which is now the site of the Rainbow Pavillion west of Kiddieland and north of the theatre. The top of the theatre can be seen to the left of the picture.

29

All the staff wore the same uniform when this picture was taken. And they had to look spick & span, too.

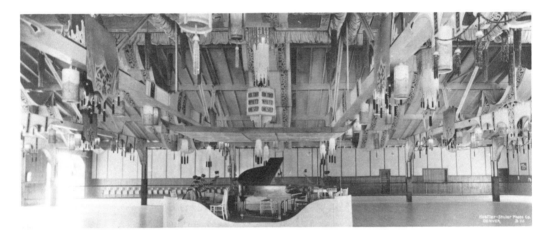

Another version of the Trocadero.

Although the Park was closed for the winter, a Christmas scene was mounted on the front gate.

THE MARVELOUS TROCADERO

Hunt: To many people, the Trocadero was what made the Gardens most special.

Gurtler: The first thing my father wanted to do when he came to the park full time was to beautify the old ballroom. Grandfather told him to go ahead. Grandfather was very fond of my father and would usually let him carry out the ideas he'd present. He would say, "Well, if it costs that much, how would it look if we spent a little more?" Nothing was too good for the Gardens where my grandfather was concerned.

This is how the Trocadero looked in 1923.

So Grandfather said, "Okay, son, go ahead and do what you wish with the thing, but make it really outstanding."

My father had heard of a fellow in Chicago who had done some exceptional decorating so he said: "I'd like to go back and spend about a week or two with him, catch on to his designs and do some things back there in Chicago with him. Then I'd come back to Denver and decorate the ballroom in the manner I feel will be the coming thing and that will be appreciated by the dancers."

So Grandfather said, "Go right ahead, son, and don't forget. If it costs $1.00, what would $5.00 make it look like?"

So Dad went to Chicago and found this fellow and he learned how to make these drawings — my father was a terrific decorator and had a great imagination. Then he came back to Denver in the early winter and hired a bunch of fellows to follow his designs and made it up sections at a time.

One of the first bands to play under the Gurtler-Mulvihill regime was the Johnny Hopkins Orchestra, a local fellow here in Denver. Following him was a guy by the name of Vic Schilling. Well, these were all local orchestras and they were doing quite well.

In 1928, J. Eddie Turner and his orchestra, outside the Trocadero.

The Company of 1933. Don Woods was the leading man, 7th from the left, and Margalo Gilmore, the leading lady, stands to his left. Jack Gurtler is third from the right.

The company of 1938. Note the man on each end; he's the same fellow — Bradford Hatton, the stage manager. Photos like this were done by time exposure, which allowed a person time to run to the other end of the line from where the camera had first been focused and appear in the same picture twice. Jack is second from the left.

The Elitch Theatre Company of 1944 when Raymond Burr was the leading man.

Freddie Martin and his orchestra in an engagement at the Troc.

The J. Eddie Tuller orchestra on the bandstand at the Trocadero.

One funny story about Johnny Hopkins — Grandfather said to my father, "Now, Arnold, this boy that's playing up there; I want you to tell him two things. He has to sweep out the place before the dance and then sweep it out afterwards." Can you imagine, telling Les Brown or Lawrence Welk or any of the bands still playing today that in order to play in your ballroom they'd have to sweep it before they could play!"

Lakeside was playing orchestras of local talent and so was the old Rainbow Ballroom downtown Denver in the wintertime. But my Dad thought, "When I'm back at the International Association of Amusement Parks, Pools and Beaches at the convention, I'm going to look around and see what other parks do that have dance pavillions."

In talking with some of these fellows, he learned that they used what they called "traveling bands." My dad asked, "What do you mean, traveling bands?" and they all explained that it meant bands from the cities — New York or Chicago — who would come in to their towns, play a weekly engagement and move on.

So my dad got ahold of a fellow by the name of Jules Stein who had a bunch of local guys there in Chicago that played in the lake area during the mer and during the winter in hotel ballrooms. Dad asked Jules Stein about bringing one of those bands out to Denver. Jules said, "My god, what do you mean? Take a band clear out to Denver, Colorado! That's a long way out there, and I haven't got a license to put bands that far away."

Dad told him it really wasn't that far and that he should go to the music union in Chicago, tell them he wanted to become a booking agent. So Jules Stein did just that. He sold the first band and from then on, he along with Billy Goodheart, his right hand man, sold bands to my father. That was the start of MCA — Music Corporation of America.

The beautiful Trocadero Ballroom after another redecoration.

Will Osborne posed for this shot in 1936.

Gene Krupa was another popular band leader in the heydey of the Trocadero.

Anson Weeks, one of the great band leaders of the "Big Band Era" who played at the fabulous Trocadero.

Freddy Martin brought his orchestra to the Trocadero frequently during the Big Band Era.

The incomparable Guy Lombardo.

The George Hall Orchestra — 1921. The harp which this band was reported to feature is not in evidence.

Well, my dad brought in a band led by a fellow named Ross Reynolds. They booked it as a great traveling band from Chicago and gave it lots of publicity and it was a tremendous hit.

The following winter, Dad and a bunch of guys, with Grandfather's permission, of course, tore down the north part of the old ballroom and built on to it to the extent that the Trocadero stood in the days that many of us still recall. And from then on, traveling bands became so important.

Hunt: There probably were some interesting stories connected with those early bands, both the local and the traveling ones. Can you tell us about some of them?

Gurtler: My father was full of stories and, fortunately he recorded a lot of his memories after he retired so I can tell you some of them.

There was a local band that Mr. Mulvihill engaged after the local musicians put the pressure on him to go back to home town boys and he took the band business back from my father for awhile. This fellow's name was George Hall and his band had a harp! No one had ever heard of a harp in a dance band and it didn't go over very well.

But the second season that Grandfather booked in George Hall a young fellow came along and asked to sing with the band. Well, that was something different, so my grandfather gave him a tryout and he had a beautiful voice. His name was Rex Tremaine. But George Hall didn't like it at all. He complained, "If you're going to put on a cafe band or a nightclub band, go get one." But nevertheless, Rex sang and the band was a big hit. It was really his singing that put the band over that year.

At one time in its colorful history, the Trocadero looked like this.

Isham Jones who made beautiful music but didn't project any personality from the bandstand.

The next year — that'd be about 1931, I think — my father got the dance business back again and he brought in a fellow named Isham Jones. Now it was greatly conceded that Isham Jones had one of the best bands in the country. They played very danceable music. But Isham Jones had no personality on the bandstand. He'd never turn around to smile at the people or make a gracious bow, or anything like that.

My father would try to get him to put a little personality into the act — ask the people what they wanted to hear, maybe, or things like that. But Isham Jones would tell him, "If you want a clown band, then go get yourself a clown band. *I'm* not going to be a clown!" But people did like his music and he went on to become one of the best bands in the country during that period of time.

They went through a series of bands, some local, some traveling ones whose names never quite became the household words that the really great ones did. And then — Benny Goodman came to the Troc!

Now Benny Goodman had started a dance program in New York called "Let's Dance." MCA thought he was the hottest thing on the street and sold the Benny Goodman band to my father for the Trocadero. Well, Benny Goodman just didn't catch on in Denver. If there were 20 or 25 couples on the floor when he played, it was remarkable.

Anson Weeks and his orchestra.

Tommy Watkins and his Paramount Elitch Orchestra was a local band. Probably they also played at the Paramount Theatre, now the only remaining theatre from the glorious past of great theatres in Downtown Denver.

41

The great band leader, Dick Jurgens when he first played at the Trocadero.

Ted Fio Rito and his orchestra were very much appreciated by the Denver dancers who flocked to Elitch's during the Great Band era.

JIMMY FEATHERSTONE
Featured With

Jimmy Featherstone was a featured singer with Art Kassel and his Orchestra at the Trocadero.

BENNY MEROFF
and His Orchestra

Exclusive Management
ORCHESTRA CORPORATION of
1619 BROADWAY
NEW YORK

Benny Meroff was a very good jazz man and had a fine jazz band when he played at Elitch's Trocadero.

The Griff Williams orchestra about to take a ride on the Wildcat in 1936.

Orrin Tucker and his orchestra in 1938.

This was the Old Grill Room off the Trocadero Ballroom where folks could enjoy a refreshing break from their dancing. The year was 1939.

Benny Goodman couldn't understand it. He'd say to my father, "Arnold, if you'd just stand across the band stand and let me know what it is I'm doing wrong — just turn your thumbs down — I'll try to change what it is I'm doing wrong."

But my Father said, "Oh, Benny, it just won't work. You've got to go."

Jules Stein thought so much of Benny Goodman that he came out to Denver himself to see what the problem was, but he had to admit that the Goodman style just wasn't making it in Denver. He pulled Benny Goodman out of the Troc and sent him to Los Angeles where he made a tremendous hit, and from then on he was tops wherever he went. But Benny Goodman bombed in Denver!

Then there was Bernie Cummings. He was one band leader that watched his crowds, and if it was a night when most people danced to a waltz, why he'd give 'em lots of waltzes. If they seemed to prefer fox trots, he'd play fox trots.

We had lights on the promenade on either side of the ballroom — the same lights that hang in the Palace Restaurant now. They would light up at the touch of a button — "Waltz," or "One-Step" or "Fox Trot" or "Two-Step." That way the crowd always knew what rhythm was coming up and if it was a fox trot crowd, why the guys would grab their partners and the floor would fill up with couples that liked to fox trot.

Harry Cool and his band opened at Elitchs early one May. That night brought a snowstorm but people came to dance anyway, and the announcer's introduction of "It's COOL, at Elitch's" was doubly correct.

Orrin Tucker had a fine musical organization and the Gardens were "proud to have him". Wee Bonnie Baker who made the song "Oh, Johnny" popular was a featured vocalist with Orrin Tucker.

Carmen Cavallaro was "a peach of a fellow" as Jack remembers him.

Will Osborne, who played the trombone, had a very fine orchestra.

Tommy Dorsey, one of the all-time great band leaders of that marvelous era.

It was still the days of a nickle a dance, and the west side of the dance floor was the stag area. Both fellows and girls would come stag, and if a fellow wanted to dance with a particular girl, he'd just go up and ask "May I have this dance, please?" There wasn't any slap in the face or any kick in the shins. It was a very honorable way to meet a girl in those days, and many a romance that began on the Trocadero dance floor is celebrating a Golden Wedding today.

There was a fellow named Bill Carlson. He had a good band, and did a lot of crazy things. He used to wear a carnation in his button hole, but they weren't real carnations. They were made of white fudge, and at some point during the evening he'd take the flower out of his lapel and eat it. People loved it!

Then there was Lawrence Welk. He wasn't as well-known in those days, but he went over big at the Troc. He'd get off the band stand and walk through the crowd, still playing his accordion. And yes, he'd stop and dance a few steps with a pretty girl, just as he does on TV today. People were just as crazy about it then as they are now. Sometimes the whole band would be out on the floor, slipping off the bandstand one after another until the bandstand was empty and all the fellows were out on the floor, still tootlin' away.

Well, as times went on, the admission to the Trocadero had to go up because the price of the bands went up and what was called the social dancing type of admission was introduced. That was paying one price for the whole

Lawrence Welk and his "mighty Wurlitzer" — Where else, but at the Trocadero?

47

Will Osborne and his Slide Music group in 1938.

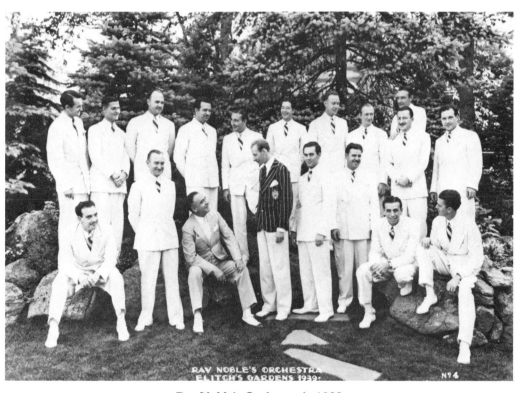

Ray Noble's Orchestra in 1939.

Clyde Lucas and The California Dons in 1940.

Bob Crosby and his orchestra in 1946. In those days, the music from the Troc was broadcast over station KFEL.

49

Another view of the Old Grill Room. The square tables for four would indicate it might have been an earlier time than the 1939 photo with round tables for two. The old fashioned "ice cream" chairs are still in evidence, however.

evening. I think the prices probably started out at $1.00 a couple — a person coming alone paid half price — and by the time the big band era ended, we were asking $5.00 a couple. Some of the band leaders would say, "You just don't charge enough here, Jack." And I'd think, "Well, we'll run the place the best we can. You just play the best music you can."

But the time came, after World War II, when the big bands were breaking up. The fellows didn't want to travel anymore. We could get a band for just one or two nights on a weekend and the rest of the time that big building was empty. It just wasn't paying its way. We could get local bands, but people wouldn't turn out for the local bands. Tastes in music changed and the younger crowds weren't into ballroom dancing.

So the day came, in the '70s when the decision had to be made that the Trocadero had to come down. It was a sad decision to make.

The last band to play in that wonderful old ballroom was Wayne King, who had been one of the most popular bands we'd ever had, and I tell you, when he played his final theme song that night nearly everyone in the ballroom was in tears — even the kids who got all dressed up for a night just to be able to say that they, too, had once danced in that great place.

Tommy Tucker's group, in 1945.

Eddy Howard & his orchestra at Elitch's in 1946. The orchestra was a frequent attraction at Elitch's after the war years and although Eddy Howard is no longer alive, the orchestra still bears his name.

LES BROWN
And His Orchestra

Personal Management
JOE GLASER

MCA
MUSIC CORPORATION OF AMERICA

Les Brown, one of the great band leaders of the Big Band Era. This early photo got the leader of "The Band of Renown" a lot of kidding. Everyone told him it was his first Communion picture.

Eddy Howard and his orchestra in 1947. The Howard orchestra was still playing the Troc in its final season, although Eddy had passed on.

The Frankie Masters Orchestra ready for a spin on the Tilt-A-Whirl — 1947.

Believe me, the day the demolition company began to tear it down was a sad day. The newspapers and TV crews were out there to record it, and when that big ball hit the north corner and the first part fell, it was like the death of a living thing. It had served it's time, lived it's life, and I'd had the honor and pleasure of sharing that life for as long as I could remember.

It wasn't an easy structure to tear down, although it was mostly stucco and wire. I'd remembered that my father told Budd and me that if we could ever get anough fellows to raise it up, we'd find that the floor was resting on horsehair cushions. I'd always thought, "Well, that's a great story from my father's imagination" but when the building came down, under the main floor there was another floor and under that second floor were those horsehair cushions.

A lot of people wanted to buy pieces of the floor or decoration for souvenirs and we let them have what they wanted. But we kept enough of the floor to build the tables now used in the Elitch Palace eating place.

We took a lot of abuse over our decision to tear down the Trocadero. I still run into people today who ask, "Jack, why did you do it?" And I have to say to them, "Where were you when we needed you? Why didn't you come out and dance to the local bands and help us keep the place going?"

But as long as people who danced there are alive, the marvelous Trocadero will live in their memories, just as it does in mine.

For a couple of winters, we ran the Elitch Delicatessen, in order to keep our good chefs. That's my brother, Budd, behind the counter.

Dick Jurgens and his Orchestra were great favorites at the Troc and came back often. This photo was the 1948 group.

Buddy Moreno & His Orchestra in 1947.

Frankie Carle and his orchestra, at Elitch's in 1953.

The Ralph Flanagan Orchestra in 1957.

MEMORIES OF THE THEATRE

Hunt: Cecil B. DeMille called the Elitch Theatre "one of the cradles of American drama." One could almost write a whole book on the theatre alone.

Gurtler: Oh yes. It has a long and fascinating history. Mary Elitch brought many famous actors and actresses to Denver, some who were just starting out and went on to become great names in the theatre later.

Cecil M. DeMille and his brother William played here in 1905. George Arliss was in that company, too. Spring Byington, Minnie Maddern Fisk, Douglas Fairbanks, Maude Fealy, Harold Lloyd, Tyrone Power, Antoinette Perry, Lewis Stone — these were all members of casts in Mary Elitch's time.

Antoinette Perry was a Denver girl and she's the one the Tony Awards are named for. Harold Lloyd and Doug Fairbanks were also Denver kids. Doug got his start by scrubbing the stage at Elitch's for the price of a ticket.

Of course, my grandfather had to learn the way to run a theatre. He'd go to New York — as did my father and Budd and I in our time — to cast the shows.

One of the New York people asked him why he didn't set up a winter company which would then help him to get the better summer shows. So he bought into the Broadway Theatre with Peter McCourt. Peter Mc Court was

George Arlis, who played in the Elitch Company in 1905.

And this man, when still a kid in Denver, got his start in the theatre by scrubbing the Elitch stage.

Some of the students in a summer ballet class.

Some of the students of the School of the Theatre and Dance at rehearsal.

One of the dance classes. These classes were free and were very popular.

Rudolph Ganz was the director of the Elitch School of Ballet during John M. Mulvihill's reign.

Harold Lloyd — another Denver boy who made it on the stage.

From left to right: A.B. De La Vergne, drama critic of the Denver Post; John M. Mulvihill; Mayro B.F. Stapelton; Rudolph Gantz who conducted the ballet school at Elitch's, Melville Burke, director at the Theatre, and Henry B. Sachs, conductor of the Elitch Symphony Orchestra.

Fredric March who defied John Mulvihill and married his leading lady, Florence Eldridge. But, she lost her job!

Baby Doe Tabor's brother, and they ran the Broadway Theatre and the Metropole Hotel (now the Plaza Cosmopolitan) together.

Well, the theatre was heated from the same boilers as was the hotel, and one winter night there just wasn't any heat getting into the theatre.

Harry Lauder was performing that night and after his first song, he said to the audience, "If this John Mulvihill can't pay his heat bill, he sure can't pay me, so you all go to the box office and get your money back. Ring down the curtain, boys! And the stage crew did just that. They rang down the curtain and the people went to the box office and got their money back.

One thing that my grandfather held to was that no leading man would be married to his leading lady. He believed that people would not pay money to watch a man make love to his own wife on stage.

Well, in 1926, the leading man was Fredric March and the leading lady was a young woman named Florence Eldridge. One day after the matinee, Fredric March came to see my grandfather.

"John," he said, "I know you've told us that in your company no one could ever be married to their opposite lead, but I've fallen in love with Florence and we want to get married."

My grandfather said, "Is that so? Well, you know what'll happen if you do."

Fredrich March with Florence Eldridge who became his wife, on his right; Florence Scheffield who became the season's second leading lady, on his left.

This cast is rehearsing in the old rehearsal lot — now the little garden area to the south of the theatre. Mel Burke, the director, is in the hat giving direction to a lady not identified and Fredrich March seated at the table.

Mel Burke was a director at the Elitch Theatre in the '20's.

Theodore Roberts

Theodore Roberts was in the Company in 1903, 1904 and again in 1905.

to right: Bottom row: Helen Luttrelle, Charles Trowbridge and Ann Masc
Idle row: Richard Carlyle, Marion Ballou, Peggy Boland and Rollo Lloyd
ow: Earle Mitchell, Albert Brown, Geo. Pauncefort, Beach Cooke, Hal Cra.

First Elitch Theatre Company Under
Management of John M. Mulvihill-1920

This was the first Elitch Theatre Company under Mr. Mulvihill's management - 1920.

Lewis S. Stone

In 1913, Lewis S. Stone was a member of the Elitch Company.

George Brent, who later got his nose straightened at Mr. Gurtler's sugges-tion. He introduced Clark Gable to Mr. Gurtler who thought that young man needed to "get his ears fixed."

Edward G. Robinson when he was in the company. Mr. Gurtler had to let him go because he didn't keep up his wardrobe!

Fredric March said, "Aw, John, you wouldn't do that to us!"

"Try me," was all that grandfather answered.

On Thursdays it was customary for the cast to have a free afternoon. The ladies would get their hair done and everyone would get their wardrobes spruced up. So on a particular Thursday, Fredric March and Florence Eldridge went to Colorado Springs and got married.

When Grandfather got wind of this, he called them both into his office, and he said, "Well, I understand that you are now man and wife."

Freddie grinned and said, "That's right, J.M.! I love this girl too much to take the chance of losing her by waiting till the season's over."

Grandfather said, "You know what I've told you. One of you has to go, and Florence, I've already engaged another lady for your part. You can stay here with your new husband, of course, but you won't be acting in the Elitch company."

Imagine! My grandfather fired Florence Eldridge because she married Fredric March! They were still married to each other when Freddie died in 1975.

In my father's time people who later made it big on the stage or in the movies came in for their share of trouble too. My Dad fired Eddie G. Robin-son because of his wardrobe! He'd warned him a couple of times about his sloppy appearance, but Eddie just didn't get around to doing anything about it, so Dad sent him back to New York. Years later, of course, Eddie G. Robinson came back as a big star and there are pictures of him in this book.

One day when my dad was in New York interviewing people for the next season's cast, a young fellow named George Brent was among those he talked to. Brent said, "Mr. Gurtler, this is a tremendous honor and I do want to be

Flobelle Fairbanks

C. Henry Gordon was in the casts of 1924 and 1925.

Flobelle Fairbanks was a Denver girl of the same family as Douglas Fairbanks, Sr. who made his debut at the Elitch Theatre.

The cast of "Quality Street" with Mary Elitch, holding the toy dog, fourth lady from the right. This would be in the mid 20's.

Ernest Glendining and Helen Menken in a more conventional pose at Elitch Gardens.

Joyce Van Patten, who played the ingenue in "Tomorrow the World" in 1944.

Ernest Glendining hams it up with one of the statues in the Gardens while Helen Mankin strikes a pose.

Interior of the Elitch Theatre with the curtain depicting Ann Hathaway's cottage in place.

The beautiful curtain at the Elitch Theatre. That's Ann Hathaway's cottage.

The entrance to the Elitch Theatre. Photos of all the great stars who've played there create an interesting before-the-show treat for guests.

a member of your company very much, because I understand that you pay your bills on time, and that you pay your cast.''

Sometimes, back East, people would open up a stock company in an old barn somewhere in New England, recruit the cast, and then go broke after a few performances, leaving the actors stranded without any pay, so it was a great plus for people to work in the Elitch Theatre because they knew they would be paid.

Well, George Brent had a friend he wanted Dad to see. The fellow didn't have an appointment, and he'd done almost nothing on Broadway, a requirement the Elitch Company had for its cast members, but George Brent pleaded so eloquently for this fellow that Dad agreed to see him for a few minutes. I've got my father's old casting notes — as well as my own and my brother's — and on that day my Dad wrote: ''I saw Clark Gable today. A very fine young man, but he ought to get his ears fixed.''

He also told George Brent after that first season that he had an awful hook in his nose, and recommended that he get it fixed before he went out to Hollywood. If you look at pictures of George Brent when he played at the Gardens and then at later pictures, you'll notice he took Dad's advice.

Another interesting story concerns the beautiful young lady my dad and Budd cast for the ingenue parts one season. She'd had very little theatrical experience except in the minor playhouses around New York and a few summer places, but she was more desirous of playing at Elitch's.

Another photo of Amy Arnell.

Amy Arnell, a lovely starlet who appeared in the 1940's.

The Elitch Theatre Company in 1929. Isobel Elsom was the leading lady to 7/13; Jessir Rouce Landis from then to the close of the season, and William Harrigan was the leading man.

The Elitch Summer Theatre Cast always tried to make a trip to Central City to see what their counterparts were doing there. This was in 1940. This is another of those photos made by time exposure which allowed Mr. Gurtler to appear at both ends of the group.

The Stock Company of 1934. The plays that year were "Men in White", "No More Ladies", "Pursuit of Happiness", "Big Hearted Herbert", "Return of Peter Grimm", "Her Masters Voice", "That's Gratitude", "Come What May", "The Shining Hour", and "Wind and The Rain". And that's Jack, standing far right.

The Cast of 1937. Ona Munson is seated second from the right. Helen Bonfils stands between A.B. Gurtler and Bradford Hatton; her husband George Somnes is seated second from the left. The plays that year were "Reflected Glory", "Hitch Your Wagon", "Love From a Stranger" and others.

She'd been here only about 10 days or so when one day a woman came to the theatre asking for this young lady. My father was called from his office by one of the stage hands, and the woman told him, "I'm Mrs. Kelly from Philadelphia and I want to see my daughter."

Mrs. Kelly probably figured her daughter was way out here in the west in some broken-down summer stock company and would end up stranded before the season was over.

In 1951 Grace Kelly's mother came out to see for herself if her daughter was playing at some seedy little theatre in the west that might not pay her and leave her stranded when the run was over. She was delightfully surprised at the Elitch Theatre and spent the summer with her daughter. Miss Kelly is seated at the left of this picture. Witfield Conner, who is the present director of the Elitch Theatre is seated fourth from the left. He was the leading man that year.

Arnold B. Gurtler with two lovely ladies — Ann Kimball and Grace Kelly.

This was one of the casts when Don Woods was the leading man. The lady in the fur jacket and bow, seated at the right of the photo is Helen Bonfils. Her husband, George Somnes is seated to the extreme right and Arnold B. Gurlter, Sr. is standing behind him.

She was pleasantly surprised at the beauty of Elitch Gardens and ended up spending the season with her lovely daughter, Grace Kelly, who went on to Hollywood to become a big star and who is now Princess Grace of Monaco.

George Somnes was our director for many years. He and Helen Bonfils were married in the Gurtler home at 38th and Raleigh — and I remember their wedding well because I got a new suit for the occasion.

In my opinion, George Somnes had forgotten more about the theatre than many present day people will ever learn.

He died the season that we built the new back of the theatre and never got to see the new backstage and the beautiful office we built for him.

I was lucky in that I got to be in some of the plays. I probably played every bellboy, chauffeur and Western Union boy that was ever written into any story those days.

I was one of the interns in "Men in White" in which Helen Bonfils played a nurse. She also played the head nurse in "The Man Who Came to Dinner" and George Somnes played the cranky guest. People really got a laugh when he'd call out from his wheel chair, "Miss Bed Pan, come in here and help me!" Although that's the way the script read, it just struck us Denverites very funny to hear the owner of the Denver Post addressed as "Miss Bed Pan."

And today, as in the early days, the outstanding talents of the theatrical world deem it a great honor to play the summer season at the Elitch Gardens theatre.

The set of "Bell, Book and Candle" in the Elitch Theatre.

One of the Elitch Company of Players being met at Denver Union Station. However the cast arrived in Denver, Elitch's personnel were on hand to greet them. Arnold B. Gurtler, Sr. is at the far right. Norris Houghton, the director, is on the left, in the light colored jacket.

74

This was a scene from the play, "My Three Angels" on the Elitch Theatre stage.

Marla Powers — a lovely actress, indeed.

Lawrence Hugo, a very talented actor, who is still active on the stage and screen.

Arnold B. Gurtler, Sr., Eddie G. Robinson and George Somnes, director of the Elitch Theatre for many years. They are here admiring the paint frame which Mr. Gurtler had created for the stage crews to work on. It was built of steel and lowered with cables into a cement cased well. It is still in use at the Elitch Theatre.

Helen Bonfils was a frequent member of the Elitch company. Denver folks got a big kick out of hearing her called "Miss Bed Pan" in the "Man Who Came To Dinner".

Douglas Fairbanks, Jr. examining some of the old photos in the theatre lobby where his father got his start.

Edward G. Robinson, reminiscing in his old dressing room upon a return visit to the theatre.

Mr. and Mrs. Arnold B. Gurtler, Sr. with Denver's own Helen Bonfils, dressed for the part of a maid in an Elitch Theatre production.

Edward C. Robinson points out a photo of himself in one of the casts in the entrance. That's my brother, Budd, with him.

Edward G. Robinson and Budd Gurtler reminisce about some of the old-time greats who played.

The three Gurtler men: Jack, Arnold Gurtler, Sr. and Budd.

FIRST FLORIST TRUCK USED IN DENVER

The first florist truck used in Denver.

ELITCH'S AND THE COLORADO CARNATION

Hunt: Probably very few people realize the big part that Elitch Gardens played in the development of the Colorado Carnations.

Gurtler: Well, of course, there are still greenhouses in the park today where we grow all of the plants used in the flower beds and hanging baskets that make our park "the Gardens". Actually, gardens were our theme long before theme parks were ever heard of. But years ago there were many, many more greenhouses and there was a magnificent smoke stack that was a North Denver landmark. That area today is part of the parking lot.

The Elitch Greenhouse Company and the Park Floral Company got together and set up a kind of co-op with other growers in North Denver and some from east Denver to wholesale flowers when it became apparent that shipping costs could be cut if everyone shipped from one central location. That was the birth of the Park Elitch Floral Company, with E. P. Neiman, president; Arnold Gurtler, my father, as vice president; John Roberts, secretary-treasurer, and Walter Lehrer as manager.

The first shop was at 1414 Wazee Street where the auto-truck entrance went through the old Denver landmark, the Elephant Corral. It has recently been renovated into a splendid office complex.

Well, this wholesale house took the time and the money to promote the Colorado grown carnations. Because of Denver's unusual number of clear days, even in winter, it was the ideal place to grow carnations as well as roses and other flowers under glass. The growers decided that one dozen of each bunch of carnations shipped should be tagged "Colorado Grown Carnation".

Whenever any of us would go to New York to book plays for the theatre, we would check out the florists there and buy only the Colorado Carnations to send to our friends, to actors or actresses we were interviewing, and to booking agents. This spread the fame of the Colorado Carnations as well as being very much appreciated by those lucky enough to get them.

When my dad was president of the International Association of Amusement Parks, he would have the wholesale house ship him a huge box of the finest carnations and he would see to it that there was always a bouquet of them on the speaker's podium every day. Of course, our suites in the hotel were always full of them, and we would share them with friends attending the convention from other parks around the country.

Later the Park Elitch Company moved from Wazee Street to 1919 South Acoma. It was a tremendous place but we needed the space as the business had grown so big.

The original directors of The Park - Elitch Floral Company. Seated, left to right: Mr. Kintzel, E.P. Neiman and Arnold Gurtler. Standing, Walter Lehrer and Mr. Roberts.

My brother, Budd, with a bunch of Colorado Carnations. The Park - Elitch Company helped make them famous across the country.

Colorado Carnations coming into bloom in one of the old Elitch Greenhouses.

It was during this period that Bill Gunesch, our field representative, teamed up with some of the fellows up at Aggies (now Colorado State University) at Fort Collins to develop a dye for carnations. Heretofore, the only dyed carnations were the green ones sold for St. Patrick's Day. They were created by sprinkling the white flowers first with a sticky substance and then with a green powder.

The new dye dissolved in water, and we'd take the white carnations out of the big refrigerated storage where they'd been held in their tightly budded stage. Put into the lukewarm dye solution in the warmer area of the warehouse, these would open almost as if by magic and turn whatever color the water they were placed in was. You could just stand there and see it happening.

The Park Elitch Company took the carnation out of the formal funeral piece which had been its chief use and made it acceptable as the corsage a young man might buy for his date to wear when he took her out dancing at the Trocadero.

But after World War II the greenhouse business gave way to the family operated truck farms and glass operations developed by the Japanese who came to Colorado. And our dear friend and manager, Harry Hoag, passed away. The greenhouses never really recovered after that, and the time came when we had to go to our father and show him the figures that said they were no longer a profitable operation. We needed the space where they were for more parking because more families were now driving out to the Gardens than were coming by the streetcars.

So, the greenhouses had to go, and with them the old smokestack with ELITCH'S painted down one side. I imagine my dad felt some of the same emotions as he watched that old landmark come down as I was to feel years later when the Trocadero fell to so-called progress.

Today what remains of the many Elitch greenhouses are used for growing all the plants you enjoy in the formal gardens and everywhere in the park, including our famous hanging baskets. On a cold winter's day, it's very pleasant to walk through the rows and rows of developing plants and feel the promise of yet another summer of beauty for Elitch Gardens.

AND THEN THERE WAS KIDDIELAND!

Hunt: Wasn't the Elitch Kiddieland something of a first for parks like yours?

Gurtler: It was after Budd and I were managing the park that we hit upon the idea of a special area just for kids. We'd been back to the convention and made arrangements with some of the ride builders there for some children's rides. We had a playground area and we planned to take it out and put in about four kiddieland rides.

Well, our dad hit the ceiling. He said, "I leave you two alone for a little while and you think you know all there is about running a park. And now you're going to tear out all that great playground area!"

We told him we knew it would work; we both had small children by then, and our wives were excited about helping launch something that children would enjoy and which would please their mothers as well. Dad thought getting our wives involved would just make a double mess of things!

But we went ahead, tore out the old swings and things and put up four rides. We added a fish pond stand and built a food stand.

The food stand was interesting because we excavated about two or three feet so that the employee was just about chest high to the counter and on an eye-to-eye level with the small customers.

The Little Chief Fire Engine from Elitch's Kiddieland. This was a fun ride for the youngsters who first came to the newly created Kiddieland.

This miniature railroad was built by Frank Root, shown here driving the engine. He had worked for Mary Elitch during her ownership of the Gardens, and he built all the rolling stock of the railroad.

This was one of the sights people saw when they rode through The Old Mill, the "dark ride" which was destroyed by fire.

Our wives, my Harry Lou and Budd's Barbara Ann, invited all their friends who had children for a free day early in June to kick off our new Kiddieland, and it's never had a dull day since. Of course it's grown a lot from those first four rides, and the children who come today are the children — and maybe even the grandchildren — of those first kids who initiated Kiddieland at Elitch Gardens.

THE GOLF COURSE

Hunt: There are quite a few young people today who undoubtedly think the greatest thing at Elitch's is the miniature golf course because it played a large role in their being able to get a college education. That's a story many people may never have heard.

Gurtler: First of all, I'll tell you about building the golf course.

Budd and I had decided we should have one, and when we talked to our Dad, he was also in favor of the project. He'd heard about a man named Cook, in New London, Connecticut, who was supposed to be the best in the business of constructing such courses, so we invited Mr. Cook to come out and look around the Gardens for the best place to put one.

Meanwhile, Budd and I had scouted the area and decided we'd like to have it in the old apple orchard near the east gate at 38th Avenue and Tennyson. There were a few small picnic pavillions there that would hold only about four or six people, and the apple trees were dying from old age.

Well, when "Cookie" as we came to call him, got to Denver and looked around, he picked the very same spot that Budd and I had chosen.

He made us a proposal and we decided he was the man to do it. When the park closed in the fall — and it was a beautiful Indian Summer that year — he came back and began to work.

Entering the Gardens from 38th Ave. and Tennyson, this was the view before the golf course replaced the apple trees.

91

This photo of the path leading to the 38th & Tennyson entrance shows the old apple trees that eventually gave way to make room for the miniature golf course.

I remember one of his first requirements was for a lot of ground up cinders. I tell you I had one heck of a time finding enough of them, but finally, by calling the steel mills in Pueblo and all the railroad yards, we did get the cinders he needed.

My, there was a lot of excavating for that golf course. I asked Cookie one day if he was digging for water, and he laughed and said, "Just hold your horses there, kid. You know I told you there had to be so many feet down below surface where I wanted to have this real hard rock put down first, and then the cinders on top of that, then sand and dirt and more fine sand on top of that."

His calling me "kid" reminds me that one day he said to me, "Would you believe that I'm 70 years old?" and when I said no, he said, "Well, I didn't say that I was. I just asked if you'd believe it!"

He spent the whole winter, just going home for Christmas, and our workers enjoyed working with him because he was the kind of guy who would tell them what he was going to do and how we were going to do it. He told us he wouldn't have put it in without guaranteeing that it would make money the very first year. Neither Budd nor I believed anything could make money the first year, but when that golf course was opened, it was an immediate success, and it's never stopped being one.

In the '70's the idea came up about having a golf tournament. Budd, John Eby, John McInery, Dick Braun, Dick Campbell and Dr. McClintock put it together and it became an annual event. Dick Campbell represented the Eisenhower-Evans Scholarship Fund and Dick Braun was associated with the Trans-Mississippi Scholarship Fund, both granting awards to students who had experience as caddies or golfers.

Budd and I agreed to contribute $1,000.00 to each fund each year of the tournament. We invited players from the major clubs around Denver and Colorado Springs, from the print and broadcast media and from public office holders.

Each participant paid an entry fee and those fees, together with the contribution made by Elitch Gardens went to the two funds. The participants designated which fund they wanted their fee to be donated to.

It was fun for everyone because we invited the golfers to bring their families — if their own children were grown-up, we included the grandkids — and admission to the park and unlimited rides were free to the families. We'd set up a 19th hold in the Tea House Pavillion with a bar and lots of hors d'oeuvres and then serve a catered dinner in the La Fonda Pavillion when the prizes were awarded to the winning teams or individuals.

Over the 10 years of its life, the Elitch Invitational Golf Tournament raised over $43,000.00 for the two scholarship funds and we are very proud of that contribution to the young people of the country.

Elitch's awaits the beginning of a new season. Though it looks asleep, hundreds of workmen are painting, repairing, improving, making ready for a future that will be every bit as glorious as Elitch's illustrious past.

Special Photos by Brad Gordon

Rare aerial view of Elitch's.

EPILOGUE

Elitch's is many things to many people. To some, the Old Orchard Cafe was special. It was a place to dine before going on to the theatre or to dance at the Trocadero. It was truly dining in a garden, with its sides open to the air and the scent of flowers and the sounds of America having a wonderful time.

Still others may remember the years when the Greats of Jazz was an annual affair in the Trocadero. From 1965 through 1969 jazz artists like Ralph Sutton, Clancey Hayes, Bud Freeman, Bob Haggart, Peanuts Hucko, Yank Lawson, Morrie Feld, Lou McGarity, Cutty Cutshall, Billy Butterfield, Gus Johnson, Bob Wilbur and Carl Fontana were part of the great sounds of Elitch's. In 1965 there were 8 Greats of Jazz and by the last year, 1969 there were 10 playing. It was a very exciting thing.

To others it is the rides that make Elitch's great, particularly the two wonderful roller coasters. The Twister is rated one of the top exciting coasters in the country by people who make a hobby of riding them. Can you believe that this is the way some people spend their vacation — traveling around to various parks just to try out the coasters, collecting the experience the way others collect trophies?

The Elitch coasters were the creation of the man who was known as "Mr. Roller Coaster," John Allen. While many of the coasters being built today are steel framed, the Twister and the Wildcat are on wooden frames, meticulously maintained, and this is part of their special charm for the coaster aficionados.

And to thousands of Denver area people, Elitch's is remembered as the place they got their first job. Summer jobs at Elitch Gardens have financed a lot of school expenses, both in high school and college, at the same time teaching what holding down a job means, affording the making of lasting friendships and having fun at the same time.

Could John and Mary Elitch have ever dreamed that what they began would still be going, stronger than ever, some 90 years later? Could John Mulvihill believe that what he saved for his city would become such a world-famous spot that the slogan, "Not to see Elitch's is not to see Denver" became the literal truth?

Yes Elitch Gardens is what it has always been — contemporary, exciting, beautiful. And its story is being written every summer when each visitor adds his own version.